YOU ARE
THEIR
LIGHTHOUSE

PARENTING GUIDANCE FOR A NEW AGE

JILL S. MacDONALD

GoWith-IN
THE SERIES

ISBN: 978-1-7355601-5-1

Edited by: Amy Ashby

Published by Warren Publishing
Charlotte, NC
www.warrenpublishing.net
Printed in the United States

"No other relationship sets the tone for the life experience of every individual more powerfully than the relationship between parent and child."

–ABRAHAM (VIA ESTHER & JERRY HICKS)

GoWith-IN
THE SERIES

Get the entire series!

Awareness. Clarity. Power
You Are Their Lighthouse
Evolutionary Relationships (Summer 2021)

Dedications

This book is first and foremost dedicated to the one who asked me to be his family—and then created one with me. I love you, Mikey. Parenting with you has been one of the greatest joys of my life. Thank you for trusting me with everything. Our kids really are the best. I'm so grateful they grew up marinating in love, and that I get to have this experience of family with you. Almost thirty years together has flown by. I can't wait to see what the next thirty brings. We are so blessed to be on this journey together.

To the ones who made me a mom:

Kailey Alison, you are my sunshine. You make me proud every single day. Your grace, enthusiasm for life, initiative, creativity, and unparalleled wisdom will carry you to all the places you want to go. I am so lucky to be your Mama! You'll always be my number one girl.

Eli Michael, you are a special soul. My buddy. Your way of being in the world has touched not only my heart, but all who know you. I have no doubt you will live your life with kindness, integrity, individuality, strength, and wisdom—as you always have. I can't wait to see the man you will be. You have my heart for always!

And to my angel (in human form) who found me fifteen years ago and helped me find my spiritual self: I became a better person and a more present mom because of that. Darin Robert, what a beautiful surprise you were! You have stood beside me (with patience and love) while I made the long journey from the mind to the heart. Alison and Dougy knew exactly what they were doing—and all the beautiful ripple effects it would create for us all. I am so proud of the mindful, centered man you have become. Turns out, I'm the lucky one! You are a part of this family for always. TMDA.

All of you helped to make me the parent I became. I am beyond grateful to be able to live out my childhood dream of being a present, relaxed, and loving mom. Being able to implement all the concepts I had about parenting and see them come to fruition is more fulfillment than I could have dreamed. And I could not have done it without all of you in my corner. You all have given me the best experience of what love is. Your love made me who I am, and this book is what it is because of all of you. Thank you!

And last, but far from least—to you, reading these words. I wrote this book to bring you more ease and confidence in your parenting journey. I wrote it to support you through the highs, the lows, the challenges, and the triumphs. Your kids are lucky to have you. I hope this book supports you every step of the way.

You've got this!

On Children

Your children are not your children.
They are the sons and daughters of Life's longing for itself.
They come through you but not from you,
And though they are with you yet they belong not to you.

You may give them your love but not your thoughts,
For they have their own thoughts.
You may house their bodies but not their souls,
For their souls dwell in the house of tomorrow,
which you cannot visit, not even in your dreams.
You may strive to be like them,
but seek not to make them like you.
For life goes not backward nor tarries with yesterday.

You are the bows from which your children
as living arrows are sent forth.
The archer sees the mark upon the path of the infinite,
and He bends you with His might
that His arrows may go swift and far.
Let your bending in the archer's hand be for gladness;
For even as He loves the arrow that flies,
so He loves also the bow that is stable.

–KAHLIL GIBRAN (1883 – 1931)

Contents

Welcome

I'm so glad you're here.

This book has found it's way into your hands at just the right time.

Whether you are a parent-to-be, a new mom, a new dad, or more of an experienced parent, this book is for you.

The journey of parenting is quite an adventure. It's love like you've never felt before and exhausting in a way you've never experienced. It will take you to the greatest joy you've ever felt, and the most frustration. It also introduces you to yourself in a whole new way.

Almost two decades into my experience as a mom, I see how much my kids have molded me into a better version of myself. They have taught me to open my heart, be more patient, more self-aware, more loving, more giving, and more self-reflective. Self-reflective, because I want to be the best version of myself for them. I want them to feel abundantly loved and to always know they can be themselves. I want not just to guide them, but to bring out the best in them. It's a moment-by-moment practice.

Being a parent has been the most fulfilling thing I have ever done. I hope that by reading this book, you will begin to feel more fulfillment and ease in your parenting experience. There are so many parents who are stressed out, spread thin, and so uncertain as to whether or not they're doing it "right."

You are doing it right.

You are doing your best.

Know how much that matters.

And now you're reading this book to enhance yourself as a parent which, in turn, enhances your kids' lives. That matters too.

So, sit back. Relax. And take in this little book of insights and wisdoms slowly. Know that you are the expert on you. Listen to your inner knowing as you read. This book is meant to gently guide you to your own awareness and clarity, so you can parent in a way that is in alignment with yourself and your family.

I hope you enjoy every page. And I hope this book brings you ease, confidence, and joy. Enjoy the journey. It is the most important thing you will ever do.

And don't let anyone tell you otherwise.

So much love,
Jill

(Parenting) will take
you to the greatest
joy you've ever felt,
and the most frustration.
It also introduces
you to yourself in a
whole new way.

Introduction

Our children choose us. And we choose them.

It is a choice made at a soul level.

It is an incredible journey of loving, learning, growing, and expanding for both parent and child. It is a powerful and sacred bond. We are inextricably linked to our children—heart to heart, soul to soul.

There is no love like the love a parent has for their child, or a child for their parents. There is no greater intrinsic trust than a child has for their parents. It is the trust of life itself. A trust that must be guarded and protected by us.

Choosing to be a parent is an enormous responsibility. That choice means taking on that deep trust they have in us to maintain their safety—emotionally, psychologically, spiritually, and physically. To parent is a blessing, a gift, an honor, and a challenge like no other. Parenting is a sacred responsibility; it is the choice to guide the formation of a human being's life.

Allow that responsibility to inspire you to be the best parent you can be.

Guiding a human being's life is most effectively done from an awakened state.

Yet somehow in the grind of our daily lives, we often lose sight of that broader awareness.

The trick to parenting in an awakened state is balancing self-awareness and self-care with lots of patience and parenting tools.

It is my hope that this book will provide you with tremendous support.

I hope you will hear my voice and feel my heart as I guide you closer to your own inner knowing. You were built for this or you wouldn't be doing it. You are exactly who your kids need. Do you know that? It is so important that you know that.

You are who your kids need because you are who they have. It is that simple and also that profound. Your kids chose you—strengths, imperfections, flaws, and all. You are exactly who they need. I hope you will feel more confidence and ease with each passing page.

Embrace the colorful experience of parenting.

And always lead with love.

The trick to parenting
in an awakened state is
balancing self-awareness
and self-care with
lots of patience and
parenting tools.

You Are Their Lighthouse

A lighthouse is both expansive and powerful.

Let's consider what a lighthouse represents, what it does, what it provides, and how it links into our place in our children's lives.

A lighthouse stands strong, grounded in its place.

A lighthouse lights the darkness, offers direction, leads the way, and asks for nothing in return.

A lighthouse knows its intention and purpose.

You are your children's stability. You are their first and most important experience of dependability. You are their light in the dark. You are their developmental guide. You are their introduction to life.

You are their Wayshower; the one who is meant to offer direction but not to *direct*. Navigation is their responsibility. Your responsibility is to be the light they can always depend on.

You have the chance to be the brightest light in your kid's lives. Be their lighthouse.

They Chose You

To feel, sense, and know that your children's souls chose you is the beginning of a long exhale.

Choosing to trust and have faith in the bigger picture of your life, and the lives of your children, means shifting into the flow of parenting. It's a complete embrace of your place in their lives and their place in yours.

You are exactly who your kids need. They just need you to be yourself. When you parent as yourself you are freed from the pressures of what a parent *should* be and can relax into who you are.

Your authenticity is powerful.

Instead of buying into the idea that you need to "live up to" a role, an idea, or some idea of parenting perfection, you can relax into your true self. Couple that with unconditional love for yourself and—by extension—unconditional love for your kids, and you've got a beautiful foundation for your family.

Are you ready to let go of the expectations you're carrying of what a parent should be?

Can you imagine the extra breathing room you would have if you were more present with yourself and your children? This is an invitation to be more authentic with yourself and your kids. It's a real opportunity to embody the love you feel for them instead of becoming a role.

Can you sense the difference?

When you decide to shed the "shoulds" and the "supposed tos," you make room to explore your deepest priorities for your family and for yourself as a parent. Doing so creates space to implement the dreams you have for your family. A lot of energy is drained when you attempt to "live up to" expectations, or get tangled in beliefs and the role of parenting, rather than focusing energy on the present moment.

Remember your kids chose you. Take some time to fully embrace who you are and relax into the parenting experience.

Relax
into the
parenting
experience.

Your Parenting Paradigm

With the extra energetic space you will have from choosing to be yourself, remembering that your kids chose you, and releasing expectations, you will be able to create your family with more awareness and clarity.

Throughout this book, you will be encouraged to design and create your own Parenting Paradigm that aligns with your values, ideas, and desires. The Parenting Paradigm you create will shape the experience your kids have of you and your family. Creating this framework will allow you to be guided by the ideas and principles that are the most important to you.

A paradigm is a way of looking at something. Therefore, a Parenting Paradigm is the way you choose to look at your parenting experience. Ask yourself: what kind of mom or dad do I want to be? How do I want to show up for my kids? How do I want my kids to experience me? What kind of space do I want to hold for them? The answers to these questions will provide the foundation for your paradigm of parenting.

The Parenting Paradigm you create will be unique to your family. There is no wrong way to do it. There is only your way. Discover, explore, define, build, and create the template throughout the experience of reading this book. Make notes. Explore yourself a bit deeper and define your highest priorities.

The Parenting Paradigm you choose will become your family's foundation.

It will also allow you to relax more deeply into the love you have for your child(ren). It allows more space for you to enjoy them. You will be able to recognize what they need most from you. You will begin to feel less stress when your Parenting Paradigm is in place. So much of the suffering in parenting comes from the ache that parents feel when they believe they are falling short. Freedom and fulfillment in the parenting experience is possible.

By releasing your (mind-based) expectations, you will be able to embody more of yourself. You will have more energy available for them and for yourself. We do not realize how much of an energetic and emotional drain expectations can be. Expectations cut you off from the inner knowing that is valuable guidance. They also create blind spots that make it more difficult to see your children for who they truly are.

Your Parenting Paradigm will create the structure that guides all of your parenting choices.

Your kids need your authenticity. They do not need you to fulfill a role. They *do* need structure. Your Parenting Paradigm will create that structure.

What do you want your Parenting Paradigm to look and feel like?

Your Home

The world you create inside your home is a sacred space. It is yours to define. And you are creating it each day, whether you're conscious of that or not. The key is to be conscious about it.

The tone of your home has a profound effect on your kids and their development. Claim that responsibility. Take time to think it through. Create what you want for your family. Write it down. Speak it aloud.

Commit to it.

What do you want the energy of your home to feel like? What do you want the foundation of your family to be built on? This is your opportunity to begin creating and setting that tone. Your home's tone is the basis for the collective experience of everyone in it. This tone is a conscious decision to prioritize a predominant vibe and support that vibe on a daily basis with choices, decisions, actions, and behaviors.

In our family, that vibe is *kindness*. And that kindness is based in abundant, generous, unconditional love and understanding. Kindness has guided, informed, created, and sustained our family for almost twenty years.

What would you like the tone to be in your home?

Take some time to reflect on aspects of your own childhood. Consider what you did and did not experience in your home environment that you needed and wanted. Consider what you did and did not receive from your parents that you wanted and needed. What would you like to carry forward into your family and what would you like to discontinue? Keep what brings inspiration and peace for your family; release what does not.

The parenting experience is a canvas for you to paint. You get to choose the colors. The more awareness you bring to the experience, the more fulfilling it will be for you.

Parenting *can* be the most fulfilling thing you've ever done. The secret is aligning your heart's desire (for your family) with your choices, decisions, actions, and behaviors on a daily basis.

Intention is very powerful.

What are your most important intentions for your family?

The tone you set in your home will support your parenting experience. It will support the highest good of your kids and your family as a unit. It aligns you with the Parenting Paradigm you have created. It helps to bring more awareness into your daily life as a parent.

The Parenting Paradigm you create coupled with the tone you set in your home, will help your kids to feel safe and supported all throughout their development. Embrace this creative opportunity to consciously create your family with intention.

Get on the Same Page

Whomever you parent with, the most important thing is to get on the same page.

That does not mean you have to agree on everything; it means that your intentions are aligned and on the same page with a similar energy and vibe. It means you agree on the tone for your home and the Parenting Paradigm you embody and implement.

Naturally, you will each bring different aspects of yourselves to your kids. That individuality is a beautiful thing and so beneficial. The two of you need to communicate about the energy you want to create in your home, what your core values are for your family, and what is most important for the kids to experience in their home.

Speaking your family's priorities aloud will strengthen your parental bond and guide you when things are challenging.

Know that the relationship you have with your parenting partner, the love you feel toward one another, how you express conflict, and how you support one another is always being observed and absorbed by your kids. Make a commitment to nurture and strengthen your relationship. The relationship the two of you have will make a strong imprint.

Your kids are beneficiaries of your relationship's strength and connection.

Speaking your family's priorities aloud will strengthen your parental bond and guide you when things are challenging.

You Are Their Foundation

You are your children's foundational start to life.

You set the tone for their experiences through your interactions with them.

You set the tone for how they feel about themselves by how you treat them.

This awareness of how your kids feel about themselves creates a paradigm shift that is a powerful game-changer. You are responsible for building and reinforcing your kids' sense of value.

Your children need you to be aligned and focused within your own authentic self. As you embody that energy on a daily basis, you create a safe container in which they can grow and develop in authenticity as well.

In a world full of confusion, conflict, and mixed messages, your children need you to be consistent, dependable, and authentic. In doing so, you create a strong foundation within them.

When you release the pressure of the parental role, and instead embrace the fullness of your being, your own foundation of self-awareness becomes stronger. As a result, you have more to offer your kids.

You are who your kids need.

You, learning right alongside them.

You in your authenticity.

You in your truth.

You, creating a space of unconditional love.

You, committed to your own self-awareness, growth, and expansion.

You, flexible and willing to see them for who they are past your expectations.

You, meeting them where *they* are each day, in each moment.

You, patient with *yourself* first, and then with them too.

You, capable of seeing the best of who they are, and holding that vision, even when they aren't being their best.

Can you feel those words? That is heart-centeredness coming alive within you.

This new awareness can be at the center of your parenting practice. It is a moment-by-moment choice to drop out of the role and into the wisdom of the heart.

Did you know that the heart holds a higher state of consciousness than the mind? The heart's electromagnetic field is sixty times that of the brain. It has even been said that the heart is the seat of wisdom.

I truly believe it is.

Release the Role

The role of parent has been built into something pressurized by society, rather than guided by each individual's inner knowing and guidance.

As a result, parents unconsciously set limitations, place pressure on themselves, create additional stress, and deny themselves the joy of the parenting experience. In turn, the kids get tangled in the weeds and miss out on the parent(s) they need the most.

Have you found yourself saying:

A good mom should do ABC?

A good dad needs to do XYZ?

Do you know who decides whether you're a good mom or dad?

It's not you. It's not society.

It's your *kids*.

Your kids are the ones who get to decide.

The only people who matter when it comes to how you parent are your kids. Their opinion matters. They *know* you. They *see* you.

Kids see their parents with the purest lens of love. They carry no judgments of you. Judgments are learned. So you must release the judgments you have of yourself first.

Your kids' natural state is to see you with clarity and love. Your responsibility is to see them that way too—organically, naturally, and without judgments.

You cannot love them and judge them at the same time. Judgment and love cannot coexist. Where there is judgment there is no love. They are opposing energies. Catch yourself when you are in judgment. Notice it. Make some space from it. Drop into your heart. Take a deep breath. Center yourself in your heart and pay attention to the difference. There will be a shift. This is a powerful transformative exercise. The more you do it, the more automatic it will become.

Kids are organically non-judgmental and unconditionally loving until they begin to experience judgment and love with conditions.

Most of us were raised marinating in judgment. Most of us experienced love with conditions. Your parenting experience gives you the opportunity to recognize your judgments (when they surface) and choose love instead. Through this choice, you heal the judgments within yourself, as you allow your children to experience a home without judgments as well.

Remember: your kids don't need perfection. They need you to just be you, who also happens to be their mom or dad.

So, take a big exhale.

Be Yourself

Know that your children want you to be yourself.

They actually need you to be yourself. They cannot learn to be themselves if you do not lead the way with your own authenticity. That means flaws and all. Continue to challenge your beliefs of what a good parent should be. Ask yourself if those beliefs are actually even yours. Question all of this at a deeper level.

Ask yourself who you want to be for your kids.

By questioning your beliefs on a deeper level, you become more aware. With that awareness, you can make alterations. This awareness is an ongoing ebb and flow throughout the parenting experience.

Ask yourself who you want to be for each of your kids and what each of them needs from you. These wants and needs will be different at each stage, so this is a question to ask yourself all throughout their development. The answer will shift as their needs shift.

Be open and fluid with your parenting practice. You will feel so much freer and so will your kids. Freedom is a big key to the happiness of all human beings—adults and kids alike.

Continue to challenge
your beliefs of what
a good parent should
be. Ask yourself if
those beliefs are
actually even yours.

Energetic Signatures

Each child carries their own unique energetic signature and personality.

Each child has different needs.

Each child expresses those needs differently.

And each child will need from you differently.

As your children need *from* you, you have an opportunity to grow within that experience. This is not always easy. Challenge any resistance you may feel toward meeting those needs as they surface. Your children's needs are not meant to be negotiated—because they are *needs*. The trick is to discern wants from needs. This is easier to do when they are two years old and under. But if you train yourself to pay close attention and become a keen observer of them, you will recognize their wants from their needs.

You may sometimes find yourself questioning whether those needs are real. You may also find yourself questioning whether or not you are willing to meet those needs. Your perception will not change their needs. It will, however, challenge you to meet those needs.

If you get into a practice of dropping into your heart and questioning any resistance you feel to meeting their needs, ideas for meeting them will come to you. This practice will also create an opportunity for you to honor *your* needs as well.

In the first seven years of a child's life, the foundation is laid for their sense of security in the world. Therefore, unmet needs during this period create insecurity. This is a time when insecurity can become a part of their energetic signatures. However, by choosing to simplify your parenting perspective, developing your Parenting Paradigm, and attending to your children's needs, they will grow into grounded, confident human beings.

Become a keen observer of your kids, take notice of what they need, and do your best.

Remember, your *presence* is their greatest need.

Presence can be as simple as putting your phone down when they ask you a question, looking into their eyes when they are upset, getting down to their level to speak to them, putting aside something important you're doing when they ask for your attention, or playing with them even when you don't feel like it.

When you become more present, you will feel more attuned to them. You will also feel more at ease when you meet their needs.

When you gently tune into your children—while simultaneously remaining connected to yourself—you align with them organically, and they will feel more understood.

Each of your children's energetic signatures serves as guidance for you as they grow and change. When you follow their rhythm and honor their flow, you will come to understand and learn more about their unique signatures.

As you come to know and understand your kids better, they come to know and understand themselves better too. You reflect back to them who they are by how you see them, treat them, guide them, meet their needs, and love them.

You are their mirror.

Their Needs

Throughout the process of exploring your children's individual needs, it is important to view their needs with a wider lens.

The real essentials are:

To be loved without conditions

To be loved generously

To be cherished

To be seen

To be heard

To be given a voice

To be understood

To be guided with gentleness and patience

To be trusted

To be safe

To be nurtured

To be uplifted

To be protected

To be inspired

To be forgiven

To be believed in

To be guided back to themselves over and over and over again.

Know that you are their lighthouse, illuminating who they are each day. Know that when you meet their most essential needs, who they are becomes illuminated. Know this is not a list of to-dos. It is an energy you embody. These essentials are part of an ongoing collaboration with your children.

Know that it's not a coincidence that the very things your kids need from you are also aspects you may need to develop more fully within yourself.

As you begin to recognize the aspects of yourself that may resist meeting their needs, you will have an opportunity to recognize the resistance you are feeling, and make a conscious choice to shift. As you allow yourself to meet those needs, you may also find yourself healing from whatever created resistance within you.

Look at yourself through your child's eyes.

There may be moments you will not like what you see. But those moments are the *opportunity*.

If you are willing to see through the eyes of your child and remember their perspective, you will see them in a completely different way. You will see yourself differently. You will be better equipped to honor who they are, meet their needs, listen, empathize, understand, see, and feel them as they are.

Be gentle with yourself as you learn to be a better parent. Gentleness is a strength … not a weakness.

Creating Harmony

We are energy.

Everything is energy.

Harmony is created in relationships with an understanding of both energy and connection.

When you come into resonance with your kids, the result is harmony. To be in resonance means you understand, feel, and attend to their individual frequency (a.k.a. vibe or temperament).

As you peel away the layers of parental expectations within yourself, develop your Parenting Paradigm, and come into more self-awareness, you will be in a higher resonance with your kids.

Our kids are born at a higher vibrational frequency than we are. Their vibration is more pure. The mistaken belief of generations is that our children are supposed to align to *us*, to adapt to us. We are actually here to understand *them*, to come into resonance with them. This allowance creates harmony within them. It also creates harmony within our relationship *to* them.

You are your kids' first relationship.

You set the first tone of what "relationship" feels like to them. Your relationship with them sets a foundation for all other relationships they will experience. That is a powerful template. Know you are creating it. Honor that responsibility.

Prioritize harmony.

When you come into resonance with your kids, the result is harmony.

The Lens of Partnership

As parents we are, in essence, our kids' very first life partner(s).

All throughout your kids' developmental years—whether you know it or not—you are partnering with them—in life, in love, and in trust. When you choose to trust them, nurture their inner voices, listen carefully, and guide them closer to themselves, you show them what real partnership is.

You partner with them by respecting their individuality, asking for their thoughts and opinions, inquiring more closely about their inner selves, and validating their emotions and feelings. As a result, they come to understand themselves better.

A lens of partnership defies the traditional concept of "parent knows best." Within that conceptual framework, kids need to be molded.

Children (and even babies) are knowing, wise, and intuitive little beings. You will discover that when you observe them closely (with neutrality), you will create space to see them for who they are separate from you. Then as they grow older, you can continue to give them permission to have their own voice. They need that permission from you.

You can nurture each of your kid's voices and their individuality more effectively when you view parenting through the lens of partnership. This immediately gives them an equal value. Why? Because a partnership lens views the relationship from both perspectives—parent and child—which forms a collaboration foundationally.

Have you ever asked yourself how you could possibly know what's best for your child if you're not inside of them? Have you ever recalled your own childhood and times when your parents thought (and/or said) they knew best but they did not?

Your children need your guidance. But they do not to be molded or indoctrinated into anything. You can't possibly know what's best for them at all times, in all ways, and in all circumstances. They are born with a strong sense of their own being. But in order for that to develop, surface, and strengthen, you need to see them for who they are, listen closely, and guide them using the lens of partnership.

As soon as you have your first baby, you realize they are so much more than a blank slate.

Children come into the world with an orientation, a personality, a temperament, and tendencies. Ask any parent about their kid(s) and they can describe attributes they have observed since their kids' infancy that exist throughout their development. Additionally, parents (of more than one child) will share how different each child is from the other(s). Therefore it is necessary to observe each child and make a commitment to see, know, and meet their individual needs as well as create an on-going partnership with them.

A strong partnership—led by you—can provide a powerful template for your kids for what a partnership is and what it feels like. Experience is the best teacher. Give them the opportunity to experience partnership with you. It will provide a template for all of their relationships. This is a priceless gift.

Family = Team

Traditionally, families are structured as a hierarchies, and the vast majority of families still function that way.

Our family doesn't. And I would like to share our perspective with you. We see our family as a team.

If you chose to be a team with your partner, when the kids arrive they naturally become a part of that team. And now that you've become parents, you become Captains of the team. Remember Captains have important reponsiblities to the team but are also members of the team.

When you choose to view your family as a team and allow it to function like one, your perspective on everything changes; everything now comes from the viewpoint of that team.

How your team is managed and how it functions is up to you. That is the creative part. It's the fun part too! Allow yourselves to be creative. Create your team *your* way. You are the Captains after all.

As your kids get older and can better understand, introduce them to team concepts. Utilize a team structure to shape and inform your family. Utilize a team structure to make choices and decisions for your family. And always keep in mind that every member of your team has a purpose, a voice, and a contribution.

Family = Team

For our family, this was one of the most pivotal choices we made. Structuring your family as a team brings out the best in the Captains and their players. It also keeps your family (a.k.a. your team) evolving and growing together.

We all have things to learn—parents and kids alike. And like a championship team, it takes a bit of magic, a bit of balance, and a commitment from every member of the team. It is a commitment to individual growth, as well as striving for your best— collectively and individually. The older your kids get, the better and stronger your team becomes.

A family that is a team needs solid leadership.

A family that is a team honors each voice on that team.

A family that is a team communicates.

A family that is a team collaborates.

A family that is a team is a powerful force of nature.

Structuring your
family as a team keeps
everyone evolving
and growing together.

Learn from Each Other

Many of our own lessons are intermixed with our children's needs, wants, and experiences.

We are soul family not just biological family. Our children are gifted to us not only to be guided by us, but for us to expand and grow alongside them. They can (and do) trigger us all along the way, which highlights where we need to grow ourselves. We can learn from them as they learn from us. But we have to be open to that learning and aware each step of the way.

As your kids grow, they will have different needs that require different aspects of you. Sometimes that's challenging. Sometimes what your kids need will require you to give up what you want in those moments. Your lesson comes in developing flexibility, fluidity, and patience. The discernment is knowing when you need to step aside and when you need to step in.

Our daughter's first few years of life marked the development of our Parenting Paradigm. We paid close attention to her signs and signals when she was a baby, followed her natural feeding and sleeping schedule, and allowed her to let us know what she needed. It got easier as she began to talk and verbally express herself. Our intention was to meet her needs and to help her to feel safe with us, and in the world around her. We noticed she had all kinds of ways to communicate to us what she felt—even before she was verbal. We noticed how capable she was to express to us exactly what she needed when we paid close attention. Our daughter taught us how to be more fully present.

We would remind one another to support her, listen to her, be patient with her, and love on her. We continued to grow ourselves, to nurture our relationship with one another, and to do our best to provide our daughter with a peaceful and loving home environment. That became the template for her (and her brother's) entire upbringing.

Learn from your kids as they are learning from you.

As your kids grow, they
will have different needs
that require different
aspects of you.

Be Aware of Yourself

Awareness of yourself comes into clearer focus when you observe how you interact with your kids, what they trigger in you, and what comes up that needs healing. This is a continuous unfolding throughout the parenting journey. It is different at each age and stage that you experience with your kids. Along the way there may be things that surface for healing from your own childhood. Just gently pay attention.

The more you bring awareness to the wounds of your own developmental experiences, the more you clear the way for your kids to have a better experience than you did.

Each generation has the opportunity to improve upon the last.

As you become an observer of yourself, you are able to catch your triggers. You are able to recognize the beliefs that create projections when you make a conscious commitment to be aware. Once you bring your attention to anything, you're able to make adjustments to it.

Continuous investigation of your own beliefs (that you adopted during your development) is key while parenting. So too is questioning what being a parent means to you, who you want to be in your children's lives, and how you choose to interact with them at each stage of their development.

Your awareness and clarity is vital to developing and engaging in your Parenting Paradigm consistently. In time, doing so will begin to feel like second nature.

Children are naturally more conscious when they live in a conscious environment at home.

When you take responsibility for your "stuff" rather than projecting it onto your kids, you protect their innocence. Projection surfaces as an outgrowth of unconsciousness. When you make the unconscious conscious, you are then able to behave with clarity and intention.

With your Parenting Paradigm defined, you can embrace a broader perspective on everything. You can embrace more wisdom.

A commitment to self-awareness is a gift not only to yourself, but also to your kids.

When you take
responsibility for your
"stuff" rather than
projecting it onto
your kids, you protect
their innocence.

Parent from the Heart

Parenting from the heart means leading with your heart's wisdom.

Can you sense that wisdom within you?

When you parent from the heart your actions, choices, and behaviors are filtered with the wisdom of the heart. It takes practice because we have become a mind-based species. This is not necessarily in our highest good. And when it comes to parenting, the heart's wisdom will connect you to your kids. Kids need to feel and experience their parents' hearts in order to feel safe and loved.

The heart offers balance. It is a place of harmony within us. Spend more time there. When you begin to practice getting quiet and dropping into your heart more regularly, you'll connect with the harmony of the heart. It is your natural state of being. The heart literally has its own consciousness. In science, this is referred to as the "second brain."

Harmony can inform your choices and decisions.

With practice, each moment will shift into a greater frequency of harmony.

Intention is powerful. Your intentions are like a snowball at the top of a hill. As it rolls down the hill, the speed is influenced by your choices, actions, and behaviors. With harmony as the intention, anything in disharmony becomes much more apparent.

Connect into your heart-centered awareness each day. Connect with the knowing and guidance you have and trust in your parental instincts. This guidance naturally lies within us all. It is a matter of getting quiet enough to sense and feel it.

Explore more of yourself from the center of your being. Take some time to go into the quiet space of your heart. Notice what being more heart-centered feels like for you. We pay so much attention to the chatter of the mind, and not enough attention to the wisdom of the heart. It takes time to make that shift.[1*]

The mind is a tool; the heart is your guide.

Human beings hold tightly to their beliefs. Notice yours when they surface. Most of us have strongly-held beliefs about parenting. These beliefs are given to us by our parents, our cultures, our religions, our societies, and our friends. Therefore, in order to know if we actually align with the

---

1 *To learn more about heart-centered awareness, read Book 1 of the GoWith-IN series, *Awareness. Clarity. Power.*

parenting beliefs we were given, we need to explore those beliefs more closely.

Most of the time, the beliefs we have about parenting come from how we were parented. That does not mean however, that those beliefs are yours, or that they need to determine how you choose to parent.

Heart-centered awareness becomes clearer once you tune in to yourself. Challenge your beliefs. Keep what brings you peace. Keep the beliefs that align to your highest self, visions, and Parenting Paradigm. Discard the beliefs that get in the way of harmony, peace, and the intentions you have for your family.

Job or Journey?

Perspective is everything.

Parenting does not have to be the hardest job you've ever done if you don't choose to look at it as a job.

To view parenting as a journey will completely change your experience. It will allow you to relax into the experience and know there is a lot to learn along the way. Your children are your teachers too. As they grow, you grow—if you allow it to happen. Your kids are your partners in the parenting journey.

Parenting is a huge aspect of your own life's journey throughout your kids development.

You develop as they develop.

You learn as they learn.

When authoritarian parenting was the norm, it no doubt felt like a job. But we have evolved from there. Now is the perfect time to view parenting through the lens of a journey rather than a job. Yes, it is a responsibility, but it is not a job.

It is an experience.

Parenting can actually be the most fulfilling thing you've ever done.

Honor your individuality. Honor the way you choose to parent. The parenting experience is not for societal consensus. It is *your* journey. It is your kids' journey too. Honor their individuality.

Honor the journey you are on together.

Parenting is a huge
aspect of your own life's
journey throughout
your kids development.

Let Go

In parenting, we experience feelings of intense attachment.

As strong as that parental attachment may be, we also need to learn to let go. It is a tricky balance. But both are needed for our children to be healthy and whole. Your kids need roots and wings. There is no exact formula. That discovery can only come from the experience you have with your kids.

That depth of love you feel for your children creates that extreme attachment and strong feelings of possession. Be mindful of that tendency. Pay attention to those feelings. The fierce protectiveness parents have can easily be confused with ownership and turn into control.

The strong and powerful love you feel can be met with fear or trust.

Control is fear. Trust is love. Trust takes practice.

The balance between attachment and letting go will be different at each stage of your kids' development. No one can tell you how to balance it. But the more you go within and listen to your inner parenting guidance, the more you will find that balance.

Trust yourself.

How you rise to the enormous love you feel for your kids—with fear or with trust—will mold their foundation. You can choose to meet your kids with love and trust over and over. Recognize when the fear comes and choose love instead.

You can choose to experience the awe of your children's individuality.

You can remain mindful that you're blessed to guide them.

You can witness their development with neutrality.

You can remember, on a daily basis, that you are a part of creating a human being's life.

The journey of parenting will challenge your ability to trust your kids, yourself, and life itself—over and over. Trust is a muscle that grows stronger over time. As you observe and witness your children's brilliance—and their inner-guidance system at work—your trust will become stronger.

When you remember that your children do not really belong to you, that they are on loan to you (because they belong to themselves), you can release the pressure on yourself.

The more you go
within and listen to
your inner parenting
guidance, the more you
will find that balance.

You Are Their Introduction

You are your kids' introduction to life.

You are their predominant experience on a daily basis. You are their mirror. How you treat them mirrors back to them who they are. The way you speak to them, look at them, hold them, support them, guide them, and listen to them informs their sense of value.

Parental love has the potential to be the purest of loves. A love that is without judgment or conditions, without injustice or games. Know that you are introducing your kids to their value by how you treat them. This is one reason why cherishing them is so very important. In order for them to feel valuable, they have to be valued.

"Cherish" is a verb. It means to treat with affection and tenderness; to treasure.

We are each born with a guidance system. Introduce your kids to their guidance systems. Call it "intuition," or call it a "gut feeling" … it is a muscle that needs time and attention to develop. Begin by asking them how they feel about situations, people, and experiences. Asking them their opinions and views throughout their development is a subtle way of highlighting to them their inner-knowing and wisdom. As they answer you, they connect to their own voice.

You can help them to develop a stronger trust in themselves and their own discernment. You have to ask the questions with neutrality to allow them the space to explore themselves more closely without your influence. Once they become aware that they have a guidance system and learn to trust it, they will have a much stronger connection to their own inner being. With that connection to their inner being, they will become more confident in themselves and their choices. In turn, you will too.

Every parent wants to know that when their kids step out into the world, they know how to make good choices and decisions. Trust that their guidance system will serve them well. It is a built-in life preserver.

You are your kids' introduction to the world.

You are their introduction to love, to trust, to their value, and to who they can be.

Be their steadiest relationship and their strongest partnership.

Be their biggest fan.

Every parent wants to
know that when their
kids step out into the
world, they know how
to make good choices
and decisions. Trust that
their guidance system
will serve them well.

Afterword

Making the choice to trust the parenting journey, your kids, and the partnership you have with them will bring you both ease and direction.

Developing your Parenting Paradigm will bring you confidence. Trust in that.

You are not supposed to know it all. You are not supposed to be perfect.

Honor your kids as individuals. Accept that you are not meant to always know what's best for them. That is for them to learn. Choose instead to be in collaboration *with* them.

Communicate early and often.

Allow their wisdom the space to express itself.

Show them that you want to hear what they have to say and value their contribution, no matter their age.

If you let them, they will amaze you.

I hope this book has helped you to feel inspired, uplifted, and guided toward your own inner clarity.

Your kids adore you.

Adore them back.

Embrace and enjoy your parenting journey.

Children Learn What They Live

If children live with criticism,
They learn to condemn.

If children live with hostility,
They learn to fight.

If children live with ridicule,
They learn to be shy.

If children live with shame,
They learn to feel guilty.

If children live with tolerance,
They learn to be patient.

If children live with encouragement,
They learn confidence.

If children live with praise,
They learn to appreciate.

If children live with fairness,
They learn justice.

If children live with security,
They learn to have faith.

If children live with approval,
They learn to like themselves.

If children live with acceptance and friendship,
They learn to find love in the world.

–DOROTHY LAW NOLTE

GoWith-IN
THE SERIES

Get the entire series!

Awareness. Clarity. Power
You Are Their Lighthouse
Evolutionary Relationships (Summer 2021)